HORSE BREEDS

# THOROUGHBRED

BY SAMANTHA S. BELL

Kids Core
An Imprint of Abdo Publishing
abdobooks.com

**abdobooks.com**



Printed in the United States of America, North Mankato, Minnesota.
052025
092025

Cover Photo: Shutterstock Images
Interior Photos: Mick Atkins/Shutterstock Images, 4–5; Cynthia Lum/Icon Sportswire/Getty Images, 7; Michael Reaves/Getty Images Sport/Getty Images, 8; Sergey Sushitsky/Shutterstock Images, 10; Sepia Times/Universal Images Group/Getty Images, 12–13; Shutterstock Images, 15, 18–19, 25, 26, 28–29; GraphicaArtis/Archive Photos/Getty Images, 16; Larisa Zorina/Shutterstock Images, 21; Lo Chun Kit/Getty Images Sport/Getty Images, 22; Eclipse/ZUMAPRESS.com/ZUMA Press, Inc./Alamy, 24

Editor: Marie Pearson
Series Designer: Ryan Gale

**Library of Congress Control Number: 2024949003**

**Publisher's Cataloging-in-Publication Data**

Names: Bell, Samantha S., author.
Title: Thoroughbred / by Samantha S. Bell
Description: Minneapolis, Minnesota: Abdo Publishing, 2026 | Series: Horse breeds | Includes online resources and index.
Identifiers: ISBN 9781098297527 (lib. bdg.) | ISBN 9798384930044 (ebook)
Subjects: LCSH: Thoroughbred horse--Juvenile literature. | Horses--Juvenile literature. | Horse breeds--Juvenile literature. | Zoology--Juvenile literature.
Classification: DDC 636.132--dc23

# CONTENTS

People cheer on their favorite horses at races.

# NECK AND NECK

It was Family Day at the racetrack. Todd and his sister Ava would get to watch a horse race! His mom packed a bag with sunglasses, hats, and sunscreen. His dad grabbed water bottles and binoculars.

Todd and his family found their seats just in time. The race was about to start. Todd's favorite horse was a brown Thoroughbred named Storm Chaser. Ava's favorite was a gray Thoroughbred named Evening Star. Todd looked through the binoculars. He could see the horses lined up at the gate.

The bell rang, the gates flung open, and all the horses took off! Todd shouted with the crowd as Storm Chaser raced ahead. The horse's legs looked like a blur as he led the others. The horses and **jockeys** rounded the first turn. Now Evening Star was catching up. As they started the last turn around the track, Evening Star passed Storm Chaser.

The starting gates open at the same time so all horses start together.

The Kentucky Derby is one of the most-watched horse races.

Evening Star kept the lead. The crowd shouted louder as the horses raced down the final stretch. Suddenly, Storm Chaser had another burst of speed. It seemed as if he would not give up. He pushed ahead in front of Evening Star. Todd jumped up and cheered. Storm Chaser won!

## Built for Speed

The Thoroughbred is one of the most athletic horse breeds. Thoroughbreds have been bred for racing. They can run at high speeds for long distances. Many Thoroughbreds can run 40 miles per hour (64 km/h) for more than 1 mile (1.6 km). They are also good at jumping.

### Happy Birthday

In the Northern Hemisphere, all Thoroughbred foals celebrate their birthdays on January 1. Even foals born late in the year turn one on January 1. In the Southern Hemisphere, foals celebrate their birthdays on August 1. This helps people keep track of which horses are allowed to race.

Retired Thoroughbreds sometimes become companion horses.

Jockeys understand Thoroughbreds. They know how to handle their energetic personalities. Each jockey and horse work together as a team to win.

The United States is the top country for racing and breeding Thoroughbreds. A baby horse is called a foal. There are about 55,000 Thoroughbred foals registered in the United States every year. Thoroughbreds that are not racing are often used in other **equestrian** sports. Some take on other roles, such as trail horses. There is plenty to love about Thoroughbreds!

### Further Evidence

Look at the article below. Does it give any new evidence to support Chapter One?

**Five Fun Facts about Thoroughbreds**

abdocorelibrary.com/thoroughbred

The Godolphin Arabian was named for his owner, Lord Godolphin.

CHAPTER 2

# HISTORY OF THOROUGHBREDS

Between 1689 and 1729, three men brought **stallions** from the Middle East to England. The horses were named the Darley Arabian, the Godolphin Arabian, and the Byerly Turk.

The men bred these three stallions with England's horses.

The new type of horse could carry more weight than the Arabians. They could run faster and farther than the English horses. The new horses became the first Thoroughbred racehorses.

## To the United States

In 1730, the first Thoroughbred arrived in the American colonies. His name was Bulle Rock. He was a son of the Darley Arabian.

### Triple Crown

Three popular US horse races are the Kentucky Derby, the Preakness Stakes, and the Belmont Stakes. A horse who wins all three wins the Triple Crown championship. The Triple Crown started in 1875, but the first horse didn't win it until 1919.

Kentucky remains the center of Thoroughbred breeding in the United States.

More Thoroughbreds came. The first Thoroughbred horse race in what is now the United States took place in Maryland in 1745.

After the American Revolution (1775–1783), Kentucky and Tennessee became the horse-breeding centers of the United States. Horse racing had become a popular activity for many Americans. Around this time, a man named James Weatherby began researching the family lines of hundreds of racehorses.

Artists painted successful racehorses in the 1800s.

Weatherby traced racehorses back to the Darley Arabian, the Byerly Turk, and the Godolphin Arabian. He published the first book with this information in England in 1791. The book became known as the *General Stud Book*. Today, it is maintained by the English Jockey Club.

Americans began keeping records of racehorses in 1868. Five years later, Colonel Sanders D. Bruce published the *American Stud Book*. He had spent years researching the family lines of American Thoroughbreds. In 1894, the American Jockey Club formed. It maintains the *American Stud Book* today.

## Explore Online

Look at the website below. Does it give any new information about the history of Thoroughbreds that wasn't included in Chapter Two?

### The History and Meaning of Jockey Silks

abdocorelibrary.com/thoroughbred

Gray horses are born dark brown or black. Their color fades as they age.

# LIVING WITH THOROUGHBREDS

Thoroughbreds come in many different colors. They may be **roan**, black, gray, or white. But almost 90 percent of Thoroughbreds are a shade of brown. Some are reddish brown, called chestnut. Others are reddish to dark brown.

They have black manes, tails, and legs. This coloring is called bay.

Thoroughbreds and other horses are measured in hands. One hand is equal to 4 inches (10 cm). Horses are measured from the ground to the top of the **withers**. Early Thoroughbreds were about 14 hands tall. Today, most Thoroughbreds are a little more than 16 hands tall.

There are basic standards for what Thoroughbreds should look like. They should have long necks. Their eyes should be far apart. They should have lean bodies with long, muscular legs.

Thoroughbreds are brave and energetic. They also have a lot of heart. This means

# Thoroughbred Colors

Thoroughbreds come in several colors. These can be with or without white markings on the face and legs.

they are competitive. They do not give up easily. A Thoroughbred's speed, ability, and determination are more important than its appearance.

Thoroughbred training centers sometimes have swimming pools to help horses build muscle for racing.

## Racing and More

Thoroughbreds can start a racing career when they are two years old. Most racehorses do their best when they are about four or five years old. Some Thoroughbreds race for a couple of years. But others will race for ten years or more.

Racehorse owners can earn a lot of money by breeding their Thoroughbreds. Breeders pay high fees to mate their female horses with winning stallions. They hope the foal will become the next champion.

## Naming Thoroughbreds

Owners often choose creative names for their racehorses. But they must follow some rules. For example, the name can be up to 18 characters long. Also, it cannot be the same name as another horse that is racing or breeding. All names must be approved by the Jockey Club.

Some retired racehorses, such as Lava Man, continue to work at racetracks. Reporters ride them while covering a race.

Off-track Thoroughbreds (OTTBs) are Thoroughbreds that were trained to race but are not racing. Some OTTBs raced many times and then retired. Some were injured and could not race anymore. Others just

Thoroughbreds can be children's riding horses.

did not want to compete. When a racehorse retires, it needs to get used to its new lifestyle. With patience and training, many OTTBs start new careers.

People of all ages love their Thoroughbreds.

Some OTTBs compete in other types of contests, such as **dressage**, jumping, or barrel racing. Others become trail-riding horses or police horses. Some are trained as therapy horses. They can help people learn important life skills. Whether racing or learning new jobs, Thoroughbreds give their best. They do well both on and off the track.

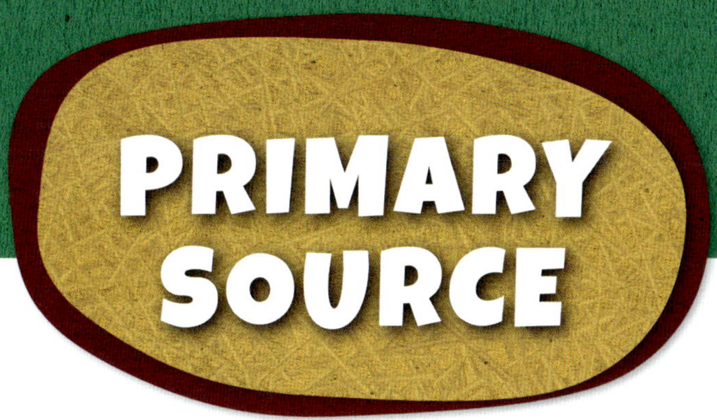


Sue Lyman trains and shows Thoroughbred horses in Virginia. She talked about careers for retired racehorses:

> Thoroughbreds that have raced and retired **sound** can hold up well as show horses. . . . Track winners usually have heart and the desire to win, qualities that transfer to the show ring.

Source: Sue Lyman. "Between Rounds: Take A Chance on A Thoroughbred." *Chronicle of the Horse*, 16 June 2022, chronofhorse.com. Accessed 4 Dec. 2024.

## Comparing Texts

Think about the quote. Does it support the information in this chapter? Or does it give a different perspective? Explain your answer in a few sentences.

# BREED TRAITS

Lean body

Wide-set eyes
Long neck
Long, muscular legs

# Glossary

**dressage**
a sport in which a horse and rider perform graceful patterns with very small cues from the rider

**equestrian**
having to do with horses

**jockey**
a person who rides horses in races

**roan**
a color with white and dark hairs mixed together

**sound**
free from injury

**stallions**
male horses who can have offspring

**withers**
the highest part of a horse's back, located between its shoulder blades

# Online Resources

To learn more about Thoroughbreds and other horses, visit our free resource websites below.

Visit **abdocorelibrary.com** or scan this QR code for free Common Core resources for teachers and students, including vetted activities, multimedia, and booklinks, for deeper subject comprehension.

Visit **abdobooklinks.com** or scan this QR code for free additional online weblinks for further learning. These links are routinely monitored and updated to provide the most current information available.

# Learn More

Cavanaugh, Neil. *Can't Get Enough Horse Stuff.* National Geographic, 2023.

Grossblatt, Ben. *Horses.* Starry Forest, 2021.

# Index



# About the Author

Samantha S. Bell lives in the foothills of the Blue Ridge Mountains with her family and four cats. She has written more than 150 nonfiction books for students from kindergarten through high school. She grew up around horses and ponies and sometimes rode them bareback.